Seasons

What Can You See in Winter?

Siân Smith

Chicago, Illinois

© 2015 Heinemann Library
an imprint of Capstone Global Library, LLC
Chicago, Illinois

Edited by James Benefield and Kathryn Clay
Designed by Richard Parker
Picture research by Tracy Cummins
Production by Helen McCreath
Originated by Capstone Global Library Ltd

Library of Congress Cataloging-in-Publication Data
Cataloging-in-publication information is on file
with the Library of Congress.
ISBN 978-1-4846-0356-7 (paperback)
ISBN 978-1-4846-0367-3 (eBook PDF)

Photo Credits
Getty images: Jim Arbogast, 11; iStockphoto: ©
PamelaJoeMcFarlane, 18; © ParkerDeen, 7; Shutterstock: ayosphoto,
20 left, Beata Wawrzyniuk, 16, BestPhotoStudio, 19, Bobkeenan
Photography, 13, Brykaylo Yuriy, 9, 22, Franck Boston, 20 right,
gorillaimages, 12, Kotenko Oleksandr, front cover, Monkey Business
Images, 5, newphotoservice, 6, back cover, Pavel L Photo and
Video, 20 middle, Pi-Lens, 14, RDaniel, 10, 22, Richard Schramm, 21,
romakoma, 17, Triff, 4, 15, Zurijeta, 8

Every effort has been made to contact copyright holders
of material reproduced in this book. Any omissions will
be rectified in subsequent printings if notice is given to
the publisher.

Contents

Things You Can See in Winter

You can see snow.

You can see snowballs.

You can see a snowman.

shovel

You can see a shovel.

You can see sleds.

icicle

You can see **icicles**.

You can see **ice skates**.

You can see hats.

You can see gloves.

You can see holly.

You can see snowplows.

You can see bare trees.

You can see wreaths.

You can see lights.

You can see hot chocolate.

You can see soup.

Winter Quiz

Which clothes would you wear in winter?

The four seasons follow a pattern. Which season comes after winter?

?

summer

winter

fall

Picture Glossary

 **ice skates**

 **icicle**

Index

Answer to quiz on page 20: hats and coats
Answer to question on page 21: spring

Notes for Teachers and Parents

Before Reading

Building background: Talk about the seasons of the year. Which season are we in at the moment? Ask children what they would see if they looked out of a window in winter.

After Reading

Recall and reflect: Which season is before winter? Which season follows winter? What is the weather like in winter? What is the best thing about winter?

Sentence knowledge: Help children count the number of words in each sentence.

Word knowledge (phonics): Turn to page 10. Ask children which word starts with /y/. Which word starts with /s/? Which word starts with /i/?

Word recognition: Have children point to the word *see* on any page. Ask children to find the word *see* on other pages.

Extending Ideas

Make a Snowflake: Give each child a square of white paper. Fold the paper in half to make a triangle. Fold the triangle in half again to make a smaller triangle. Position the triangle with the point down. Fold in each side toward the point. Cut off the top of the folded paper at an angle. Now cut out large shapes from the sides of the triangle. (Children may need help with cutting as the folded paper is thick.) Have children open up the triangle to reveal their snowflakes. While making the snowflakes, have children identify shapes.

In This Book

Topic Words
gloves
hats
holly
hot chocolate
ice skates
icicles
lights
shovels
sleds
snow
snowballs
snowmen
snowplows
soup
trees
wreaths

Topic
Winter

High-frequency Words
a
can
see
you

Sentence Stem
You can see _____.

Ask Children to Read These Words:
hats p. 11
gloves p. 12
hot chocolate p. 18